Fuelling Performers

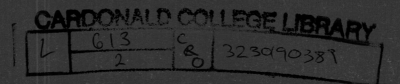

sports coach UK is the brand name of The National Coaching Foundation and has been such since April 2001.

ISBN-13: 978-1-902523-23-7

Author
Jeanette Crosland

sports coach UK
114 Cardigan Road
Headingley
Leeds LS6 3BJ
Tel: 0113-274 4802
Fax: 0113-275 5019
Email: coaching@sportscoachuk.org
Website: www.sportscoachuk.org

Patron: HRH The Princess Royal

Published on behalf of **sports coach UK** by
Coachwise Business Solutions
Chelsea Close
Off Amberley Road
Armley
Leeds LS12 4HP
Tel: 0113-231 1310
Fax: 0113-231 9606
Email: enquiries@coachwisesolutions.co.uk
Website: www.coachwisesolutions.co.uk

sports coach UK will ensure that it has professional and ethical values and that all its practices are inclusive and equitable.

This handbook is an introduction to sports nutrition. It will help you to advise performers on eating and drinking for health and sport. It both recaps and develops material from the sports coach UK Develop Your Coaching workshop 'Fuelling Performers'. However, it is also intended for those who have not attended the workshop.

For performers to enjoy sport and achieve their best results, it is important for them to maintain their own good health. Following the basic principles of good nutrition will help them to do this.

The book explains how sports performers can gain an extra advantage by making sure the food and drink they consume is not only healthy, but also gives them the maximum energy for training, competition and recovery. It will give you many tips for helping to improve the nutritional habits of your performers and discusses some of the practical issues that can commonly arise in sport.

This book will help you to:

- classify the basic nutrients
- apply the nutritional principles associated with healthy living
- advise performers on how food and drink can affect their performance
- recommend appropriate foods and drinks to your performers prior to, during and after training and competition
- identify issues and situations which may cause particular problems to the performer and know who to contact for advice.

Throughout this pack, the pronouns he, she, him, her and so on are interchangeable and intended to be inclusive of both men and women. It is important in sport, as elsewhere, that men and women have equal status and opportunities.

Contents

CHAPTER ONE:
Introduction

1.0 Why Nutrition is Important

Why is nutrition so important for sports people, fitness and exercise enthusiasts and indeed, anyone who is intent upon leading a healthy lifestyle? There are some basic facts regarding nutrition that need to be understood in order to answer this question.

Why do we Need Food?

- To provide energy for the body to function – keeping the heart, brain, lungs and other organs ticking over.
- To provide energy for us to move about.
- To help the growth and repair of muscle and body tissue.
- To help the body avoid and fight infection.

The links between health and nutrition have become increasingly apparent in the last few years. It is now recognised that heart disease is associated with a high fat intake and particularly a diet that contains too much animal fat. Diets that do not contain sufficient fibre are known to be associated with bowel problems such as constipation and possibly bowel cancer.

Media attention to health and nutrition (and beauty and nutrition) related issues has meant that people are generally more sensitive to information about their food than ever before. For those who combine an exercise regime or participation in sport with an active lifestyle, the importance of good nutrition is even more pronounced (see Chapter Three). For sports performers with high ambitions, nutrition is now given due recognition and attention alongside other performance factors such as speed, flexibility, self-confidence and team cohesion.

1.1 What is Healthy Eating?

Most people now have access to a wide range of both fresh and convenience foods. What makes a healthy choice? Healthy eating often conjures up images of lettuces and lentils, of boring food which you are told is good for you but is no fun to eat. Healthy eating does not mean boring food. A healthy diet should contain plenty of variety and be interesting. Indeed variety is one of the key factors to a healthy diet – it means eating more of many types of food and less of others. Healthy eating is choosing the right combination of foods to balance your intake and promote overall health.

The main principles of healthy eating for the population overall are to:

- eat more starchy high carbohydrate foods
- choose lower fat foods
- eat more foods high in fibre.

In addition, the following foods should not be taken in excess:

- sugar
- salt
- alcohol.

Do These Guidelines Apply to Sport?

On the whole they do. Active people need to take large amounts of foods high in carbohydrate. They should also choose the lower fat alternatives and high fibre foods. Those who are very active will find they sometimes need to use sugar or sugary foods to top up their carbohydrate intake if they have high energy requirements.

Salt should be avoided by anyone with high blood pressure. However, few performers are likely to have this condition and those who do should seek further advice (see page 48). Salt in excess is not recommended for anyone, regardless of whether or not they take part in sport. Most sports performers do not usually have excess salt in their diets as the foods they are recommended to eat (eg high carbohydrate, high fibre, low fat) are generally not high in salt. Those who rely on higher fat processed foods (eg take-away foods such as burgers, cheese slices, crisps) are more likely to have excess salt in their diets as these foods generally contain a high level of salt.

Alcohol and sport do not fit well together. While a healthy diet for most people can contain small measures of alcohol, it is recommended that ideally sportspeople avoid alcohol completely. This is because alcohol will adversely affect aspects of performance, particularly concentration and coordination. It also causes dehydration – this means it takes away the vital fluid the body needs in order to function most effectively.

Sport and other physical activity places a heavy energy demand on participating individuals. Your performers may take part in competitions or training which last several hours and where their effort has to be maintained throughout the whole session. Choosing the best source of energy for sport is therefore very important.

Have you ever wondered why a marathon runner sometimes *hits the wall* after about 90 minutes? This is partly because the body's supply of glycogen (the fuel that the body uses primarily for energy production in the muscle) will last about 90 minutes during steady exercise. A marathon runner needs to eat enough foods high in carbohydrate to provide sufficient energy for the type of exercise. If the energy runs out, the marathon runner has to stop. This example and others are explained further on in this resource.

1.2 How This Book will Help You

Those who take part in sport or who lead active lifestyles need to be healthy. Poor health will impair fitness. Active people also need to make sure they have enough of the right kind of fuel (fast fuel) – the type that will be available when it is needed. As a coach, you should know how to advise your performers on some general nutritional issues and also where to find expert advice. Remember that nutrition should be included in the planning, preparation, participation and recovery programme. This book will help you to learn about healthy eating habits. It will:

- explain the principles of nutrition

- identify the nutrients in food, their purpose, and how to achieve the right balance

- help you to understand the nutritional needs of your performers

- discuss some of the important practical issues around eating and sport.

> **Remember: A fit, healthy performer needs a healthy coach, so read this book and take a look at your own habits!**

CHAPTER TWO:
Introducing Nutrients

2.0   What is Nutrition?

Nutrition is simply a description of the foods we eat that provide us with the nutrients we need to go about our daily activities (see panel on page 1). Nutrients can be divided into the following groups:

- Carbohydrate:
  Found in starchy foods (eg pasta, bread, rice, cereal) and sugary foods (eg sweetened drinks and confectionery).

- Fat:
  Found as visible fat (eg butter or margarine) or hidden fat (eg in pastry, cakes).

- Protein:
  Found largely in meat, poultry, fish, cheese, eggs, milk, beans, lentils and nuts.

- Fibre:
  Found in cereal foods (eg wholemeal bread and cereals) as well as fruit and vegetables.

- Vitamins:
  Only needed in small amounts, found in many foods.

- Minerals:
  Only needed in small amounts, found in many foods.

- Fluids:
  For example, water and water-based drinks.

Most of the foods we eat contain a mixture of nutrients. The key to eating well for health and sport is to include a variety of foods from each of these groups.

Energy

Practically all the food people eat provides energy. This energy is usually referred to in terms of calories (or kilocalories) or kilojoules – the metric version. The energy is provided by the carbohydrate, fat and protein fractions in the diet. Each of these nutrients gives a different amount of energy, and some types of energy are more important to health and sport than others. The total energy intake should be such that it maintains people's ideal body weight.

2.1 Carbohydrate

Carbohydrate provides fuel for the body. It is used by the muscles and the brain. As well as helping the body to function, it also provides energy for exercise. Foods high in carbohydrate should account for a large proportion of the diet.

Carbohydrate can be divided into two types – simple or complex. It is not a case of either/or – sportspeople need a combination of both these types of carbohydrate.

Complex carbohydrate foods tend to be high in vitamins, minerals and sometimes fibre. This type of carbohydrate is found in starchy foods such as bread, pasta, rice, potatoes, breakfast cereals, scones, bagels and other foods made with flour, beans and lentils.

Simple carbohydrate foods are usually refined, highly processed and may contain insufficient vitamins, minerals and fibre. This type of carbohydrate is found in sugars. This group includes sucrose (the common white sugar we use at the table), glucose and fructose (fruit sugar). Simple carbohydrates are found in sweets such as boiled sweets and pastilles, soft drinks and fruit. Sugar is also found in foods such as cakes, biscuits and chocolate, although these foods can be high in fat as well. Many processed foods contain sugar – if you read the labels of tins and packets you will find it is even added to some savoury processed foods.

2.2 Fat

The body also uses fat as a source of energy. Fat actually provides more energy (calories) per gram than carbohydrate does, but it takes a much longer time for the energy from fat to be available to the body.

Fat is made up of units called fatty acids. Some of these fatty acids are needed to produce chemicals, which are vital to the body for a whole range of processes. Fat is also a source of the fat-soluble vitamins needed by the body. It is therefore important to recognise that the real meaning of a lower fat diet, is just that. There is no such thing as a true fat-free diet – people should never aim to take fat completely out of their diet.

Types of Fat

There are several different types of fat, some of which are more beneficial than others. All types of fat contain the same calories and an excess of any type of fat will lead to a gain in weight.

Saturated fat is the type known to cause cholesterol to be deposited in the arteries. This is linked to an increased risk of heart disease. It is obviously important to avoid large amounts of this type of fat. It is found in foods of animal origin including for example:

- lard
- butter
- cheese
- cream
- full fat milk
- cakes, biscuits and pastries.

Unsaturated fat is usually divided into polyunsaturated and monounsaturated fats. This simply refers to the chemical make up of the fat. Good sources of unsaturated fats include:

- sunflower, soya and corn oil
- olive oil, rapeseed oil
- margarines made from the above oils
- oily fish such as mackerel, kippers, pilchards and salmon.

Unsaturated fat does not cause the same harmful effect as saturated fat. It is therefore recommended that people use foods containing unsaturated fat rather than those with a high saturated fat content. Some unsaturated fats found in oily fish and olive oil for example, are thought to have a slightly protective role within the body as they may protect against heart disease.

Trans fatty acids are produced when liquid oils are changed into solid fats.

There is a small amount found naturally in meat and dairy products, but most is found in processed foods such as biscuits, cakes and pastries, margarines and spreads. It is thought that trans fatty acids may be harmful to the body (in terms of causing heart disease) and large amounts should therefore be avoided.

2.3 Protein

Protein is needed for the development of muscle as well as bone and skin. It also helps to maintain and repair muscle and other body tissues. However, since many foods contain some protein, most people eat more than enough to cover their needs, even during training.

Good sources of protein include:

- chicken
- meat
- turkey
- fish
- eggs
- milk
- yoghurt
- cheese
- nuts
- beans
- lentils
- Quorn, tofu and other vegetarian products.

Vegetarians need to make sure they replace the animal sources of protein with a vegetarian alternative (eg tofu, beans or lentils instead of meat, fish or poultry).

The high protein foods listed on page 6 are not the only foods which contain protein. Foods high in carbohydrate (eg bread, rice, pasta and breakfast cereals as well as some vegetables such as peas, sweetcorn, broad and butter beans, and a whole range of other bean varieties) all contain protein.

Protein is made up of amino acids and it is important to include as wide a range of amino acids in the diet as possible. This is easy to do by making sure you eat a variety of foods. Those who do not eat meat should include as much variety of different protein sources as possible in each meal, as this mixture will make sure all the necessary amino acids are present. For example, beans on toast or breakfast cereal with milk are snacks that include a variety of protein sources.

2.4   Fibre

As dietary fibre (roughage) is not actually absorbed by the body, it is often ignored. It is, however, an important part of the diet. Fibre is basically the non-digestible material that forms the skeleton of plant cells. Milling or peeling removes the outer layers of plant foods and much of the important fibre is lost. It is therefore important to eat wholemeal products (eg wholemeal bread) and the skins of vegetables (such as carrots and potatoes) so the maximum amount of fibre is maintained in the diet.

A lack of fibre in the diet has been linked with several diseases such as constipation and bowel problems, cancer, diabetes and heart disease. The official term for dietary fibre is now non starch polysaccharides (NSP) and you may see this phrase on food packets or information about nutrition. The normal recommended average requirement is 18g per day.

Fibre can be found in:

- wholemeal bread
- granary or multigrain breads
- high fibre white bread
- brown rice
- brown pasta
- baked beans and other beans
- lentils
- vegetables
- fruit – fresh, dried or tinned
- foods made with wholemeal flour
- nuts
- seeds
- porridge
- high fibre breakfast cereals (they often have fibre in the name or are brown in colour).

While fibre is important for health, there are times when too much fibre could be a problem for performers. If daily energy and carbohydrate requirements are high, a lot of fibre may be consumed and the use of some lower fibre foods might be advisable. For example, consider the long distance runner on the days leading up to a marathon. During *carbo loading*[1], the runner may not be able to take in all her bread and cereal as wholemeal varieties without causing an over-active bowel. She may therefore choose to use white lower fibre versions instead.

2.5 Vitamins and Minerals

Vitamins and minerals do not provide energy, but they are vitally important as they have very specific functions. They are taken from food in very small amounts. There is no need to supplement a well-balanced diet with tablets of vitamins and minerals, unless for medical reasons. However, if the diet is considered to be unbalanced, then the reason for this should be sought and corrections made. A supplement will not sort out the whole problem and large amounts of many vitamins and minerals are harmful.

Vitamins

Vitamins have a regulating role in the body. They are needed to trigger or control various metabolic processes, and each vitamin has a definite role. There are two types of vitamins:

- **Fat soluble vitamins** (A, D, E, K) which dissolve in fat and are stored in the body. Because they are stored, large amounts can become toxic.

- **Water soluble vitamins** (C and B vitamins) which dissolve in water. They are not stored in the body and a regular supply is needed.

One of the most effective ways to ensure a good intake of vitamins is to include five portions of fruit or vegetables each day.

1 Marathon runners are recommended to eat a high carbohydrate diet prior to their event to give them the maximum amount of energy possible.

One portion might be:

- one fruit (eg an apple/orange/banana)
- one small glass of fruit juice
- two tablespoons (80g) of cooked vegetables
- one dessert bowl of salad.

Frozen vegetables are as nutritious as fresh, but canned fruit and vegetables do lose some nutrients, so people should not rely on them all the time. Table 1 gives the function and source of vitamins:

*Table 1: Vitamins –
their function and source*

Vitamin	Function	Good Sources
A Retinol or carotene	The process of seeing in dim light. Helps to maintain skin. Antioxidant – helps prevent tissue damage.	Eggs, liver, cheese, oily fish, green and brightly coloured vegetables such as carrots.
B1 Thiamin	Carbohydrate metabolism and nervous system.	Red meat, wholemeal bread and cereals, nuts, peas and beans.
B2 Riboflavin	Carbohydrate metabolism, vision, skin and nervous system.	Milk and dairy products, eggs, yeast extract, green vegetables, meat.
B6 Pyridoxin	Carbohydrate, fat and protein metabolism, formation of red blood cells, nervous system.	Liver, eggs, fish, wholegrain cereals, bananas, yeast extract.
B12	Maintains the nervous system, production of red blood cells.	Meat, poultry, fish, eggs, cheese, milk, fortified breakfast cereals, normally found only in foods of animal origin.
Folic Acid	Production of red blood cells, healthy pregnancy.	Liver, green vegetables, nuts, peas and beans, yeast extract.
Niacin	Energy production.	Meat, dairy foods, cereals.
C	Wound healing, fighting infection, absorbing iron.	Citrus fruits, kiwis, green vegetables, tomatoes.
D	Healthy bones and teeth.	Exposure to sunlight, oily fish, fortified margarine.
E	Protects against tissue damage (antioxidant).	Vegetable oils, wholemeal cereals, egg yolks.
K	Blood clotting, wound healing.	Liver, green vegetables.

Minerals

Minerals have many functions within the body. Some help to regulate metabolism while others form part of the structures of bones, teeth, enzymes and hormones. They are vital even though they are only needed in very small amounts. Some minerals, usually referred to as the *trace elements* (such as copper and zinc) are required in exceedingly small amounts as their name suggests. Eating a varied diet is the easiest way to ensure a good intake of all these minerals. It should be remembered that excess intakes can be detrimental to health.

Two minerals in particular merit further attention – iron and calcium.

Iron

Iron is needed for the formation of haemoglobin in blood. This carries oxygen around the body. A low level of circulating haemoglobin is referred to as iron deficiency anaemia. The early symptoms of anaemia include tiredness, headache, poor performance and sometimes light-headedness. Those most at risk from anaemia are:

- females
- teenagers
- sports performers who undertake a tough training programme
- vegetarians.

Women are most at risk because of menstrual losses, but men can and do also develop anaemia. For some people iron supplements may be necessary, however, they should only be taken under a doctor's instruction as some can cause constipation and excess iron can interfere with the function of other minerals. Chapter 6.5 explains why sports performers may be prone to iron deficiency anaemia. It outlines major sources of iron in the diet, and gives practical tips for those performers who may be at risk.

Calcium

Calcium intake is important for the formation and repair of bones and teeth. Within the body there is a continual process of calcium being deposited in the bone and removed. During early life (until people are in their 20s or 30s) more calcium is deposited than removed.

In later years more calcium can be removed than deposited. This can lead to **osteoporosis** or thinning of the bones. It is essential that people have a good dietary intake of calcium during their early life, and maintain the level of calcium in their diet, to help the body replace calcium through life. While osteoporosis is more common in women, a small number of men can also develop this condition.

Lightweight female performers can sometimes cease menstruation. The hormonal effect of this can make an individual more likely to suffer from osteoporosis, even from a young age.

W. RUDLING

This means dietary calcium is even more important if this condition is to be avoided.

For most people, one pint of milk (or equivalent) a day will ensure they have the majority of the required amount of calcium in their diet. Low fat milks contain just as much calcium as full fat ones.

Some alternatives to a 1/3 pt of milk include the following:

- One pot of yoghurt
- 180g rice pudding
- 28g (1oz) of cheese
- 340g (12oz) dried apricots
- 300g (3 small pots) of fromage frais
- 84g (3oz) dried figs (five)
- 350g (12(oz) cottage cheese
- 560g (1lb 4oz) broccoli
- Two canned sardines*
- 34g (1(oz) sesame seeds
- 250g (9oz) canned salmon*
- 56g (2oz) pilchards*
- Eight slices white/brown bread

- 16 slices wholemeal bread
- Two fruit scones
- 200g (7oz) sunflower seeds
- 500g (just over 1 can) baked beans.

* Pilchards and sardines include small bones, salmon includes small bones but not a backbone.

NB As some of these quantities are large, you may need to consume them in smaller portions.

For example, instead of eating a whole can of baked beans in a day, you can eat four slices of white/brown bread and half a can of baked beans in the same day. There are many food options to ensure your diet contains the required amount of calcium.

Table 2 outlines the function and
source of minerals:

Table 2: Minerals – their function and source

Mineral	Function	Good Sources
Calcium	Formation and repair of bone and teeth, nervous system and blood clotting.	Dairy products, soft bones of fish, fortified white flour products, beans, green leafy vegetables.
Iron	Red blood cell formation and oxygen transport.	Liver/kidney, red meat, fortified breakfast cereals, wholegrain foods, green leafy vegetables.
Zinc	Metabolism of carbohydrate, protein and fat, wound healing, immune system.	Meat, dairy products, wholegrain cereals, seafood.
Magnesium	Energy production, bone formation, muscle movement.	Dairy products, cereals, vegetables, fruit.
Selenium	Protects against cell damage (antioxidant).	Shellfish, wholegrain foods, offal, meat.
Potassium	Fluid and acid-base balance, nerve conduction.	Fruit, fruit juice, vegetables, wholegrain foods.
Sodium	Fluid and acid-base balance, nerve conduction.	Salt, cheese, processed foods, cereals and sauces, bread, bacon.

Fluid

Water is an important constituent of the human body. It is found in a number of foods but it is also necessary to drink plenty of fluid to replace that lost as waste, and through sweating and breathing. Adults need a minimum of one and a half to two litres of fluid each day; those who regularly train and take part in sport need more.

Task

The easiest way to make a very simple assessment of an individual's food intake is to look at a food diary and compare what is written down with the guidelines. You could try doing this for one of your performers or even yourself now. If you do this with one of your performers, you may need to read through the information and check whether the diary includes enough detail about quantities and portion sizes. The following questions should help you evaluate the food diary you are assessing:

- Check for each of the nutrients – are all the groups represented?

- Do the high carbohydrate foods make up the majority?

- Is fat kept under control?

- Are there sufficient portions of fruit and vegetables?

- Is there sufficient variety to ensure a good mixture of vitamins and minerals?

CHAPTER THREE:
Eating and Drinking for Health

3.0 General Guidelines

The ideal distribution of the different nutrients in our diet is represented in the following chart and figures (see Figure 1).

The figures show that at least 47% of the total energy in our food should come from carbohydrate, which is the recommendation for general good health. In Chapter Four, when the emphasis shifts from guidelines for the general population to what is required for sports performers, you will notice this percentage increases.

3.1 Getting the Balance Right

A simple way to get the balance right is to look at an average plate of food. Figure 1 shows how the recommended nutrients should be distributed.

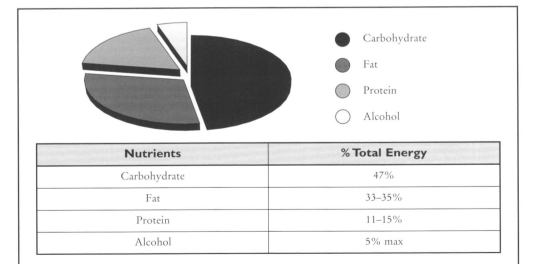

Nutrients	% Total Energy
Carbohydrate	47%
Fat	33–35%
Protein	11–15%
Alcohol	5% max

Figure 1: Percentages of total energy required for health

Approximately half of what you see should be the starchy high carbohydrate foods. This means including good portions of pasta, rice, potato, bread or breakfast cereals with each meal. There should be a good proportion of fruit and vegetables, and the fatty/more sugary foods should make up a minor section of the plate. Protein foods do not normally need to account for a large proportion as in our western society they are usually on the high side. Those who choose to follow a vegetarian diet should make sure they have replaced the animal products with a vegetable substitute such as beans, lentils, Quorn or tofu.

It is important to avoid too much fat as this is not helpful either to health or performance and excess fat will provide excess calories resulting in weight gain. Some sources of fat in

the diet are visible and therefore easy to recognise – such as spreading fats (butter, margarine or other spreads), oil, lard and fat on meat. Other sources, described as hidden fat, are harder to recognise. They include foods such as cream, pastry, pies, chocolate, cheese, the fat inside meat and fatty foods (eg sausages).

3.2 Reducing Intake of Fat

There are a lot of ways to cut down on fat intake. Some suggestions include using:

- a lower fat milk such as skimmed milk (which has all the fat removed) or semi-skimmed milk (which has half the fat removed)

- low fat or virtually fat free yoghurts or fromage frais as an alternative to full fat yoghurts or cream

- low fat or light spreads as these contain half the fat of butter or margarine

- lower fat cooking methods (ie grill, roast, casserole, boil, poach, steam – use a pressure cooker, microwave or slow cooker as opposed to fry)

- starchy snacks or fruit rather than crisps or other high fat snacks – see Chapter Four for more ideas.

As some sources of protein can be high in fat, it is also a good idea to:

- choose leaner cuts of meat

- remove the skin from chicken and poultry

- use lower fat cheeses such as edam, gouda, brie, and camembert (cottage cheese is very low in fat), or the special low fat varieties

- opt for the low fat versions of milk and dairy foods such as yoghurt.

Task

Is your diet high in fat?

Identify the major sources of fat in your diet or your performer's diet and find two ways of decreasing it. If you or your performer eat a very healthy diet, you may not be able to do this!

3.3   Fruit and Vegetables

In Chapter 2.5, it is suggested that five portions of fruit and vegetables should be taken each day. Some people feel that this is a lot to take, but the following meal plan shows how easy it is to do.

Portions of fruit/vegetables

Breakfast

Glass of pure orange juice	1
Cereal and milk/ toast	

Lunch

Sandwiches with a dish of side salad	1
Scone	
Apple	1

Evening meal

Meat, chicken, fish or vegetarian alternative	
Two cooked vegetables (2 tablespoons of each)	2
Dessert	

3.4 Barriers to Healthy Eating

Whether your performers are recreational or elite, there are certain factors that may prevent them from eating an optimum diet – you need to bear these in mind. The sort of factors may include the following:

- Cooking ability:
  Do they have the basic cooking skills? Don't presume.

- Peer pressure:
  Fruit and vegetables might not be in fashion with friends.

- Time:
  School, work, training, families, other sports all take up time and food might not seem to be a priority.

- Travel:
  Planning and preparation is needed.

- Habit:
  Do their families eat healthily?

As the coach, you need to be sensitive to these issues. However, by discussing them with your performers and their parents/guardians, you may well be able to resolve some of them.

Remember – without health, performance won't happen!

CHAPTER FOUR:
Eating and Drinking for Sport

4.0 Why Sports Performers Need Fuel

During sport the major nutritional considerations are the need for fuel and fluid.

The energy to participate in sport comes from carbohydrate and fat. Protein may be used as an energy source in extreme conditions, for example towards the end of a marathon race or very long training session, but it remains a minor contributor to total energy. Although we have large supplies of energy from body fat (even the very slim), it is only available to the body at a very slow rate. The more intense the exercise, the faster the fuel needs to be available. Therefore carbohydrate stored as glycogen is the best choice of fuel.

Fuel Use in Different Sports

The type of fuel used for different sports will vary. Here are some general guidelines:

- **For moderate intensity sport** – the body uses carbohydrate and fat.

- **For lower intensity sport** – the body uses an increased amount of fat.

- **For higher intensity sport** – the body uses an increased amount of carbohydrate.

The body always needs a small amount of carbohydrate to provide the immediate energy to keep going. Even in longer events the amount of carbohydrate stored as glycogen is the limiting factor. Once this has all been used and the body is relying on fat and protein for energy, the performer tends to have to slow down and only use energy at the pace at which it is being released. This is what happened to the marathon runner, mentioned previously in Chapter 1.1. *Hitting the wall* was the point at which glycogen stores were running out.

Carbohydrate, therefore, is the most important source of energy during sport because it is digested and absorbed quickly by the body. It is used as a fast source of energy to the muscles and brain and is stored as glycogen in the muscles and liver. It is the high performance fuel needed by people taking part in sport.

The amount of energy stored as glycogen will last for differing lengths of time depending on the intensity of the sport being done. However a *full tank* of glycogen can last somewhere in the region of 90 minutes of continuous steady exercise depending on individual factors such as training status, body size. It is therefore important for performers to eat enough large quantities of carbohydrate to maintain sufficient fuel supplies for the exercise they are doing. Many performers will train for 90 minutes at a time, including those who take part at a recreational level. Even training for an hour is fairly demanding on the supply of glycogen available to the body and recreational performers may not start with a full tank.

Dietary Recommendations for Sport

Chapter Three focuses on the dietary recommendations and guidelines for the general population. These are designed to maintain health. The recommendations for sport are similar, but because carbohydrate is so important as a fuel in sport, the amount needed in the diet is higher. This is illustrated in the following chart and figures (see Figure 2):

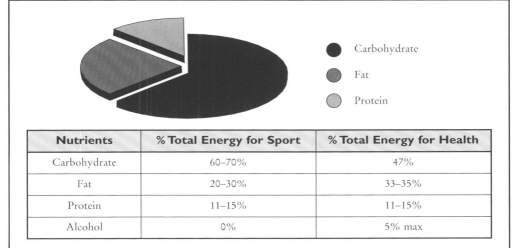

Nutrients	% Total Energy for Sport	% Total Energy for Health
Carbohydrate	60–70%	47%
Fat	20–30%	33–35%
Protein	11–15%	11–15%
Alcohol	0%	5% max

Figure 2: Percentages of total energy required for sport and health

Figure 2 on the previous page shows a larger slice of the energy coming from the foods high in carbohydrate and how this affects the recommended total distribution of nutrients in an average plate of food.

4.1 Carbohydrate

Considering the amount of carbohydrate as a percentage of the total energy intake is the easiest way to describe the quantity of carbohydrate needed by an active person. The plate model is a very good way of quickly gaining an idea of the proportions of nutrients within a certain meal, snack or daily diet. However, for more accurate individual advice, expert sport dietitians/ nutritionists will be able to be more specific about the amount of carbohydrate needed for a particular sport, taking into account individual training requirements and normal daily activities.

Performers who train regularly would normally need to include at least 6g carbohydrate for every kilogram of their body weight. During heavy training or in the build-up to an endurance event, this requirement could increase to 10g per kilogram of body weight. Performers who need

this type of detailed, specific information are advised to seek more professional advice (see page 48) – prescribing diets with this degree of accuracy takes time and practice.

If your performers ask you for some general advice about their diet, you need to consider the proportion of carbohydrate and fat in their diet. The plate model is a good way of doing this. The meals of an active person should contain large portions of foods high in carbohydrate such as:

- pasta
- rice
- potato
- bread
- breakfast cereal.

Your performers will also need advice on what type of snacks they should include in their diet. Snacks that contain a lot of carbohydrate include:

- jam or honey sandwiches
- breakfast cereals
- fruit
- dried fruit.

More ideas for snacks will be given in Chapter Five.

4.2   Glycaemic Index

The glycaemic index of a food refers to how quickly the food is turned into glucose in the blood stream. How quickly the blood sugar rises and falls varies with different foods. The rate is compared to a standard based on either the rate for glucose or white bread. The figures are similar but not identical. High glycaemic index foods include white bread, glucose and cornflakes. Foods with a lower glycaemic index include lentils, porridge and milk. The last meal before sport (this should be around 3–4 hours prior to the start of the activity) should contain mainly low glycaemic foods. However, immediately after sport, foods with a high glycaemic index are useful because of their faster absorption rate. Some performers consider the glycaemic index of a food when deciding what to eat, but great care is needed as the values cannot be used when two or more items of food are eaten together.

4.3   Fat

In order for performers to accommodate a large amount of carbohydrate in their diet, they need to find ways of reducing their fat intake. There are many ways of doing this and individuals should look at

their own diets to decide which ways would work best for them. Some ideas can be found in Chapter 3.2.

The concept of eating more carbohydrate is perhaps more appealing than the idea of having to avoid too much fat. This is an area where you may well have to encourage your performers to comply. There are a number of good reasons for performers to take this information on board:

• If performers increase carbohydrate without taking care with fat they will simply gain weight!

• Adding fat to a meal will reduce the availability of the carbohydrate by slowing down the breakdown and absorption of the food.

• The higher the volume or intensity of training, the more carbohydrate is needed. Eating too much fat may prevent performers from being able to eat as much carbohydrate as they need.

You can encourage your performers to follow a higher carbohydrate/lower fat diet by:

• using the examples of peers for whom the strategy works

• leading by example – even if you no longer compete!

4.4   Protein

For a long time sports performers thought that protein was the most important nutrient in their diet. They thought that eating platefuls of eggs and steak would build and fuel their muscles.

Performers have a higher requirement for protein than inactive individuals because of the increased protein turnover as a result of training. However, even those undertaking power sports do not need vast quantities of protein.

It is important to remember that training develops muscle. While some protein is needed for growth and repair, the most important nutrient for muscle development is carbohydrate. This will provide the energy for the high intensity training that is needed to develop muscle.

Endurance athletes need on average 1.2g to 1.4g of protein for every kilogram of body weight. In strength training this figure rises from 1.2g to 1.7g per kilogram of body weight.

Performers, who need this type of detailed, specific information are advised to seek more professional advice (see page 48) – prescribing diets with this degree of accuracy takes time and practice.

4.5   Fruit and Vegetables

Most performers are familiar with the idea that carbohydrate is important. Many will be making at least some efforts to take sufficient carbohydrate on board. Fruit and vegetables remain the poor relation in the diet of most of the population, not just those involved in sport. It must be stressed, however, that the vitamins provided by fruit and vegetables are essential for:

• turning food into useable energy

• preventing infection

• repairing the damage caused by training

• recovering from injury.

NB Fruit and vegetables also contribute to the carbohydrate content of the diet. They are an important part of the nutrition for sport jigsaw.

4.6   Fatigue

Fatigue occurs when the energy being used exceeds the energy available. Running out of carbohydrate is a major factor in the cause of fatigue. Once the body's store of glycogen has been depleted, the muscles try to cover their energy needs by burning fat but this cannot be done fast enough to meet the energy requirements.

Marathon runners experience this mismatching of the rate of energy expenditure and the rate of energy replacement. They refer to this phenomenon as *hitting the wall,* and cyclists call it *the bonk.* It is the point of fatigue when muscles feel weak and heavy. The situation is made worse when glycogen stores have been used up as the muscles then take more glucose from the blood. This reduces blood glucose concentration to a low level (known as hypoglycaemia) and prevents a regular supply of glucose to the brain. Hypoglycaemia contributes to the feelings of exhaustion.

During sport, the onset of fatigue can be delayed by starting the activity with a good supply of glycogen stored in the muscle. Chapter Five outlines some strategies for doing this. It is also important to consider the role of fluid, as dehydration is a further cause of fatigue during sport.

4.7   Fluid

Anyone who has taken part in sport is familiar with the feelings of thirst that physical exercise produces. As a result, most people drink during and/or after sport. However, waiting until you feel thirsty before drinking can lead to a loss of performance and possibly dehydration. It is essential that performers begin their activity fully hydrated and take steps to rehydrate during and after exercise.

Being dehydrated means there is less fluid available for the circulation of blood and urine, and for sweat production. It also means the heart has to pump harder to maintain adequate circulation. As a result performers may feel light headed, weak or nauseous. Headaches are one of the first symptoms of dehydration and muscle cramps can also be associated with an imbalance of fluid and electrolytes.

Dehydration can result in poor performance – research has shown that performance can be impaired by as much as 20% if 2% of the body's total weight is lost. To lose 2% of his body weight, a 50kg performer only needs to lose 1kg, and for a 90kg performer the figure rises to 1.8kg. Every kilogram lost represents 1 litre of fluid lost and it is very easy to lose this amount of fluid in a training session or a competition. It is also important to remember that speed, strength and stamina are not the only factors that can be affected by dehydration – it can disrupt concentration and coordination too. Dehydration can therefore affect all sports.

The ultimate effect of excess dehydration is death – the importance of fluid cannot be underestimated.

What and When to Drink

Water will replace fluid, but when exercise continues long enough to use considerable amounts of energy, it is useful to include a small amount of carbohydrate in a drink to boost energy levels. However, if the carbohydrate content of the drink is too high, the body will not be able to remove the fluid from the stomach and into the blood stream where it is needed. The following types of drink are commonly used for sport:

- Isotonic drinks have carbohydrate levels of roughly 5–8% (ie 5–8g carbohydrate per 100mls of drink). This is sufficient to provide a little extra energy during exercise but not enough to impair the absorption of fluid. Sodium (salt) is present to assist the absorption. These drinks can be used before, during or after training/competition without compromising hydration. This makes them a good all-round drink for sport.

- Hypotonic drinks usually contain salt and carbohydrate but in smaller amounts than in an isotonic solution. They do not provide sufficient energy to make a noticeable contribution to energy levels during exercise. However, they can be useful during very hot conditions where hydration is the most important factor and energy is not a major concern (eg short events in very hot climates).

- Hypertonic drinks have a much higher concentration of carbohydrate (more than 10%). These drinks provide energy but hinder hydration. They may be useful after training/competition

Isotonic drinks can be bought readily, but those on limited budgets can make similar alternatives at home using the following:

- 60g of glucose or sugar made up to 1 litre with low calorie squash or sugar free flavouring, plus 1/5th teaspoon salt.
  NB If the performer normally buys a glucose polymer powder (sometimes referred to as a malto dextrin), up to 100g of this may be used in place of 60g glucose.

- One part fruit squash made up with 4 to 5 parts water plus 1/5th teaspoon salt to every litre.

- Pure fruit juice diluted 50:50 with water plus 1/5th teaspoon salt to every litre.

when energy is needed but solid fuel is hard to eat. They are often used for very long endurance events (eg cycling), although it is important to balance hydration against fuel requirements.

Isotonic drinks are perhaps the most useful types of drink as they can be taken before, during or after exercise without harm. Other types of drink may not be as effective or may hinder hydration. These need to be used with great care.

Drinking Strategies

Encourage your performers to establish a drinking strategy that works for them. However, they should not rely on drinking when they feel thirsty. They need to practise drinking strategies during training and competition so they know how much fluid they can handle during sport and how quickly they can absorb it. Large amounts of fluid are actually well absorbed but they will probably make performers feel uncomfortable.

After reaching the stomach, fluid must pass into the blood stream, where it can travel to the brain and act as a coolant.

There are a number of factors which may affect the absorption of fluid from the stomach once it has been consumed:

- A high sugar or carbohydrate content in a drink means that it will be absorbed more slowly from the stomach.

- Some research has shown that colder drinks are absorbed more quickly. Certainly they are more appealing to the performer and it is likely that more fluid will be consumed if the drink is chilled. However, ensuring the temperature of drinks in a competition or even a training session can be very difficult.

- If a drink contains sodium (salt), it will be absorbed more quickly. Commercial sports drinks contain salt but if your performers are making their own sports drinks, encourage them to include a small amount of salt (about 1/5th of a teaspoon per litre of drink). If they complain about the taste of the drink, it is usually because too much salt has been added.

NB While sugar is an important source of energy in sports drinks, it can be harmful to teeth. Performers are therefore recommended to clean their teeth regularly and maintain good dental hygiene.

CHAPTER FIVE:
Putting Principles into Practice

5.0   What do Performers Need to Consider?

Sports performers spend many hours planning and preparing for competition so they can peak at the right times. Dedicated performers will also carry out strict routines before, during and after training/competition to give themselves the best possible chance of achieving their top performance. For instance, to make sure they are physically ready for training/competition and to prevent injuries from occurring, they will always go through a warm-up routine.

Nutrition should be given the same consideration as other performance disciplines. It affects how people feel mentally and physically, which can in some cases make the difference between winning and losing.

To help your performers' nutritional habits work for them, here are some tips you can advise them to follow. They need to appreciate that different principles may apply for different situations. Therefore, they should consider what to do:

- before, during and after training
- before, during and after competition.

5.1   Tips for Training

In sport, a major role of nutrition is to support the demands of training. Performers need appropriate training to maximise their performance.

It is therefore essential to begin training with an adequate carbohydrate supply and ensure that this is maintained. The rest of this section advises on how this can be done through following certain principles before, during and after training.

Before Training

- Ensure the day-to-day diet contains a large percentage of carbohydrate.

- The majority of main meals should contain high carbohydrate foods (eg pasta, rice, potato, bread, breakfast cereal).

- Use lower fat foods and cooking methods to keep fat intake lower.

- Have a main meal 3–4 hrs before training if possible.

- If the time between eating and training is too long, eat a high carbohydrate snack 1–2 hrs before training.

- Ensure an adequate fluid intake every day. For most individuals this is at least 2 litres a day plus extra, depending on sweat losses due to heat, exercise or both.

- Immediately prior to long training sessions, drink as large a volume of fluid as possible. Theoretically this could be around 600mls but it will need practice.

During Training

- Maintain fluid intake by drinking whenever the opportunity arises. 1–1½ litres an hour is possible – the most fluid achieved is usually in the region of 100–150mls every 10–15 minutes.

- Practise drinking during training – drinking and sport don't always come naturally.

- Include some carbohydrate in drinks if the extra energy would be useful.

- During long sessions (eg during sports such as tennis and cycling), it may be possible to eat small amounts of solid food to maintain energy levels.

After Training

The body is best able to begin the refuelling process during the first two hours after exercise and to take full advantage of this, refuelling should begin immediately. The muscles must be replenished and prepared for the next training session. The amount of carbohydrate needed can be calculated by body weight, but the average amount of carbohydrate to aim for is 50g immediately post exercise. The panel over the page gives some ideas of how this amount can be achieved. Younger or smaller performers may find that a slightly smaller portion would be more acceptable.

Portions of food containing approximately 50g carbohydrate

- Three slices of bread or toast
- Two slices of bread and a banana
- Two slices of bread with jam, marmalade or honey
- 2–3 bananas
- 70g (2–3oz) raisins or currants
- 400mls isotonic sports drink (7% carbohydrate) and one large apple
- 65g jelly babies/wine gums.

Rehydration should also begin immediately after exercise. Performers may not always feel like drinking large amounts after sport but drinks containing a little salt should encourage them to drink more.

It is very important for your performers to make sure they can eat the right type of foods at the right time. High carbohydrate foods may not always be readily available at training sites so it is important for performers to pack their own foods if they know this may be the case. The following kit-bag foods may be useful for training sessions and/or competitions:

Snacks to Pack

- Fruit (eg bananas, apples, satsumas, pears, grapes)
- Dried fruit (eg apricots, sultanas, dates, bananas, currants, raisins)
- Tinned fruit
- Sandwiches (eg jam, honey, marmalade, banana)
- Teacakes, hot cross buns, bread sticks, muffins, Scotch pancakes, Swiss roll, fruit cake, malt loaf, iced finger buns, Chelsea buns
- Crunchy or chewy cereal bars – try to purchase the ones with the lowest fat content
- Fig rolls, Garibaldi biscuits, digestives, ginger snaps, Twiglets
- Breakfast cereal and low fat milk (dried low fat milk can be carried), Pop Tarts, Nutrigrain bars
- Low fat rice pudding (tinned or instant) instant desserts, low fat yoghurt
- Pasta or rice salad
- Isotonic sports drinks or diluted squash.

5.2 Tips for Competition

Sports performers need good nutrition to help them cope with the demands of competition and achieve their optimum levels. The principles of nutrition for training (Chapter 5.1) also apply for competition. The major differences during competition are:

- timing of events – plan food around the day's timetable

- nervous tummy – pack plenty of choice to allow for butterflies

- venue food – performers should carry their own food as the food at sports venues is often not ideal.

Here are some tips for making sure that the competition circumstances do not hinder the performer's intake of fuel.

Before the Event

- Never try anything new on the day of a competition.

- Practice the routine before competition wherever possible.

- Aim to eat a high carbohydrate meal 3–4 hours prior to the beginning of the event.

- Carry enough snacks (see panel on page 28) to ensure appropriate food is available at a time that is suitable.

- Ensure an adequate fluid intake in the days leading up to competition. For most individuals this is at least two litres a day plus extra, depending on sweat losses due to heat, exercise or both.

- Immediately prior to long duration competitions, drink as large a volume of fluid as possible. Theoretically this could be around 600mls but it will need practice.

During the Event

- During an event of 1–2 hrs (eg a football match), drink fluid before the start, during the game where possible and at half time.

- During a shorter event that is repeated throughout the day, drink small amounts continuously throughout the day and eat small snacks (see page 28) whenever possible/necessary.

- During an endurance event, drink before the start and at regular intervals throughout the event.

- Use an isotonic sports drink to provide energy as well as fluid.

- If the sport allows and the performer is comfortable eating during play, small amounts of solid food may be sometimes be appropriate during an event (eg between end changes in tennis).

After the Event

Refuelling after competition is just as important as refuelling after training and the same principles apply. Begin fuelling as soon as possible. Use snacks and drinks to begin the process and aim for approximately 50g of carbohydrate (see page 28) every two hours until a main meal has been eaten.

A Typical Food Diary

It is almost impossible to give guidelines for the ideal diet on the day of competition. The ideal diet depends on many factors – for instance, the performer's age, sport, build, performance requirements, personal likes and dislikes, ambitions (eg world champion or club champion?). The following table (Table 3) shows a typical example of a club rugby player's intake of food during a competition day. The end panel gives comments on the suitability and timing of the food intake. It also offers suggestions on how this person could improve their nutrition.

This table is not a definitive guide for all sportspeople. For instance, gymnasts or martial arts experts may have very different requirements. As you go through the table, try to consider how the principles may relate to your sport (eg if your sport involves multi-round competitions, you will probably need to recommend more snacks and snack meals as opposed to large lunches or dinners). The purpose of this example is to show you how you can begin to analyse your performers' nutrition and the sort of advice you might offer them.

NB For more expert advice, you are recommended to consult a qualified sports dietitian/ nutritionist (see page 48).

Table 3: Example diet of a club rugby player (with comments)

Time	Activity/ Meal	Content	Comments/Recommendations
9am	Wake-up		
9.30am	Breakfast	Three slices of bacon, two eggs, two tomatoes, three slices of toast	More carbohydrate needed. Quantities will depend on the size of the performer – a large bowl of breakfast cereal with low-fat milk, plus 2–4 slices of toast with jam would be a much better choice. Some fluids should be included with breakfast.

Time	Activity/Meal	Content	Comments/Recommendations
11.00am	Snack	Two cups of coffee with two chocolate biscuits	Coffee can have a dehydrating effect so include some water, squash or sports drink instead. Chocolate biscuits are high in fat so include some lower fat alternatives (see page 28) such as malt loaf.
1.00pm	Lunch	Large bowl of pasta with tomato sauce, chicken and vegetables. One banana with low fat custard. One glass of orange juice.	Good choice of food but too close to the warm-up and the match. Take lunch earlier and either refrain from snacking or have a lighter snack. Remember to take fluid even if you decide not to snack. Banana with custard may not be necessary for some people at this stage, but this depends on their body size and appetite.
2.30pm	Warm-up		Pre-game fluid (eg a sports drink) should be included at this stage.
3.00-4.30pm	Match	One pint of water at half time	Sports drinks containing carbohydrate and salt would be a better choice.
5.00pm	Drinks	One pint of water, two pints of lager	Rehydration and refuelling needs to take place as soon as possible after the match (ie preferably from 4.30pm). 500mls of sports drink would begin both these processes. Carbohydrate should be taken at the rate of 50g every two hours. Straight after the match, two slices of bread and jam would be sufficient. Alcohol dehydrates the system so preferably this should not be consumed. However, drinking water prior to the alcohol will have helped rehydration to begin.
7.30pm	Dinner	Pizza and chips, with ice cream	This meal is rather high in fat. A full meal should be included as soon as possible after the game. This should include a mixture of nutrients (as recommended on page 19) such as chicken, fish or meat; potatoes, rice or pasta; vegetables; fruit crumble for dessert. Rehydration should continue so drinks should be included.
10.30pm	Nightcap	Coffee	Coffee dehydrates so an alternative drink would be better. Possibly include another starchy snack (see page 28) to ensure that muscles are refuelled for training the next day.

TASK

Consider your own sport. Are there issues within that sport which may cause problems from a nutritional point of view? For example:

- Do you enter competitions that last several days?
- How will your performers find suitable food over that period?
- Are there ways you could help?

Take some time to think of ways you could help your performers by advising them how to prepare for competition.

The key to eating for competition is to PLAN and PRACTISE.

CHAPTER SIX:
Practical Issues

6.0 Which Nutritional Issues Affect Sport Performers?

Within each sport there are issues associated with nutrition that are particularly important and those that cause certain problems. This chapter looks at some of those issues and offers practical advice on dealing with them.

6.1 Children in Sport

Children should enjoy sport – those who do often enjoy more than one sport. For example, they may be training with you for athletics but at school they are playing tennis and badminton, and at home, football for fun. Children also use a lot of energy while growing and it is often difficult for them to eat sufficient food to fuel their activities and their growth. They often need to eat continuously and therefore need to take frequent snacks.

For further details on children and how they respond to exercise, you are recommended to the sports coach UK Develop Your Coaching workshop 'Coaching Children and Young People' and the handbook *Coaching Young Performers* (see pages 45 and 46 for further details). It is important

to understand some basic facts about children (eg they are not as responsible as adults – they need to be told very clearly what they are supposed to do; they lose heat more quickly than adults). These types of characteristics will affect the advice you give them. Your role as a coach will undoubtedly involve careful liaison with parents or guardians as well as the children.

Tips for Children
- Check meals are not being missed to fit in sport.
- Ensure snacks are included to provide enough fuel and nutrients.
- Encourage low fat, high carbohydrate snacks for health and performance.
- Be prepared to compromise occasionally. Saying no to crisps or take-aways completely may stop them listening altogether. Aim for the best balance you can achieve.
- Check drinks and snacks sent by parents are used and not taken back home.
- Encourage them to eat plenty of fruit and vegetables.
- Lead by example!

6.2   Weight Management

Weight management is important for all sports people but particularly so for those involved in categorised weight events (eg boxing). Many performers worry about their body weight and percentage of body fat as it is a well-known fact that too much fat can hinder performance.

It is possible to estimate the percentage of body fat through various tests. Some performers are very keen to find out their scores so they can compare them to those of other performers and what is recommended for their sport. Percentage body fat figures, however, should be used cautiously as there will be inaccuracies in the readings if different people take the measurements, if different equipment is used or if the person taking the measurements is not experienced. Measurements of body fat are perhaps most useful to show changes in measurements rather than actual values.

NB You are advised to seek professional assistance for measuring the body fat of your performers. This is not only to ensure the readings are as accurate as possible but also to avoid any ethical misconduct or allegations. Body fat measurements are not usually recommended for children as there are so many variables to consider while they are growing (eg have they gone through puberty?).[1]

Individuals will gain weight as fat if they consume more energy (calories or joules) than they expend. Some individuals can consume larger energy intakes and not gain weight. This phenomenon may be due to differences in **basal metabolic rate**.[2]

---

1 For further information on child protection issues, you are referred to the sports coach UK Develop Your Coaching workshop 'Safeguarding and Protecting Children' and the home study pack *Safeguarding and Protecting Children* (see page 45 for details).

2 Basal metabolic rate (BMR) is a person's minimum rate of energy use needed to maintain life. It can be taken when a person has a normal body temperature and is completely resting. The average rate for adults is 1200–1800 kcal per day. This figure can be affected by age, gender, body size and body composition.

Losing Weight

When trying to lose weight it is important to remember the body can only lose fat at the rate of approximate 1kg per week maximum. Therefore rapid weight loss is not beneficial to the body as lean tissue (muscle) may also be lost. It is important to remember that performers at all levels need to ensure they are consuming sufficient food, especially carbohydrate, to allow them to train at their required standard. Weight loss needs to be relatively slow and steady. The major principles of nutrition already discussed in this book should be maintained. The panel below shows a few extra areas the performer might consider.

Cutting out meals or reducing intake too drastically will not help and is very likely to hinder training and performance. If specific information or advice is needed, seek professional assistance (see page 48 for further details).

Making Weight

For some people, the problem is gaining weight, not losing it. In the past it was thought by many that large quantities of protein were needed to gain muscle mass. What is needed is the correct training. It is training (and genetics) which will determine the muscle mass of the individuals.

Check that fat intake is not too high:

- Check their diet avoids any high fat foods such as cream, chocolate, fried foods, pastry, crisps, oily dressings.
- Make sure they use a low fat spread instead of regular butter or margarine.
- Make sure they always use a low fat milk.

Check for excess energy intake that could be reduced:

- Is alcohol regularly a feature of the diet? This could be reduced or cut out.
- Are restaurant/café meals a problem? Analyse the choices made and suggest better alternatives.
- Do weekends mean a change of habit – more snacks maybe?
- Are higher fat take-away foods being used?

The role of the diet is to provide the nutrition that allows the individual to carry out the necessary training. As extra energy is required, more food must be consumed. Power training is a high intensity activity and uses large amounts of carbohydrate as a fuel. This means a large proportion of the food taken should be high in carbohydrate. A certain amount of extra protein is needed, but most of this will be provided by the larger amounts of food eaten. Huge quantities of meat or other protein and supplements are not necessary – just a good appetite! Here are a few guidelines for controlling weight gain:

- Aim to gain weight gradually – the increase will probably be slow and is often difficult. Ideally any weight gain should be lean/muscle mass as opposed to fat. However, in practice, it is common for a certain amount of fat to be deposited – as training progresses, this body fat should decrease as muscle is developed.

- Follow a high carbohydrate diet as recommended for all sports.

- Increase energy intake by around 500 kcals a day.

- It may be necessary to avoid too many high fibre foods because of the bulk.

- High carbohydrate drinks may be useful to reduce the volume of food.

6.3   Eating Disorders

Within the UK generally there is an increasing problem of people trying to achieve weights that are too low for health. Coaches need to be sensitive to this when advising performers about weight loss. They need to be aware of the following common eating disorders and how to look out for possible symptoms so they might be avoided.

What is an Eating Disorder?

An eating disorder is:

a persistent disturbance of eating or eating related behaviour that results in the altered consumption or absorption of food and that significantly impairs physical health or psychological functioning. This disturbance should not be secondary to any recognised medical disorder or any other psychiatric disorder. **Fairburn and Walsh, 1995 (p135).**[1]

1   Fairburn, CG and Walsh, BT (1995) *'Atypical eating disorders'*. In Brownell, KD and Fairburn, CG (ed) *Eating Disorders and Obesity: A Comprehensive Handbook*. London, Guildford Press, pp 135–140. ISBN: 0-89862-850-4.

Eating disorders might occur in the following forms:

- **Anorexia Nervosa**
  Those suffering from anorexia nervosa refuse to maintain weight at a suitable level and have an intense fear of gaining weight, even when underweight. They will starve and often vomit or take laxatives to maintain this low weight.

- **Bulimia Nervosa**
  This is a syndrome of bingeing and purging. Binges will involve taking in large amounts of food and happen in a manner that is out of control. Sufferers may vomit, take laxatives or over-exercise to prevent weight gain. They may appear to be of normal weight or even slightly heavy.

- **Disordered Eating**
  This may include individuals showing some of the signs and symptoms of anorexia nervosa and bulimia nervosa without being clinically diagnosed as having them. It may also include those who have an excessive concern over body weight, a fear of eating fat or a target weight below an ideal for health. Look out for these signs so you can try to prevent them turning into serious eating disorders.

Who Are at Risk?

Those who suffer from these problems usually have a very strong character. They have a will to succeed, are single minded and focused – all the characteristics which could make them good performers. Many will be female, but males do suffer from eating disorders too.

There are many, often complex, reasons why individuals develop eating disorders. However, it is important to be cautious in commenting on an individual's body size and to be aware of the issue within the sporting world. Treatment can be very difficult because sufferers are often not willing or able to admit to the problem.

How Can You Help?

There are a number of general guidelines you can follow to encourage your performers to eat the right foods for their health and their sport:

- Give performers some sound, general information about sports nutrition.

- Always emphasise the importance of healthy eating for sport.

- Encourage performers to eat sufficient nutrients to cope with their training and competition needs.

If you are worried about an individual, seeking the help of a psychologist, general practitioner or sports dietitian may be helpful. There are a series of leaflets aimed at the performer, coach and carer that can be obtained from the Eating Disorders Association (see page 48 for further details).

6.4 Supplements and Ergogenic Aids

There are literally thousands of products on the market which claim to enhance performance. These might include:

- carbohydrate supplements
- sports drinks
- vitamin and mineral supplements
- ergogenic aids.

Carbohydrate supplements can be included in sports drinks. They are used by some performers to increase carbohydrate intake without increasing bulk. In this context they can be quite effective (see page 24 for more information).

Sports drinks can be a useful source of energy – see page 24 for further details.

Vitamin and mineral supplements are not necessary for those who have an adequate, well balanced diet. Performers who think they may lack sufficient vitamins or minerals should have their whole diet reviewed, as taking a supplement will not necessarily ensure adequate nutrition (eg carbohydrate and fluid should also be considered). If performers have an adequate vitamin and mineral intake, there is no evidence to suggest that a supplement will enhance their performance. (See Chapter 2.5 for more information.)

Ergogenic aids are substances that are claimed to enhance performance. Some of these are blatantly illegal (eg steroids). Indeed, many believe anything that enhances performance to a higher level could be deemed illegal. There are a number of factors performers should consider before even thinking of taking any performance enhancing substances:

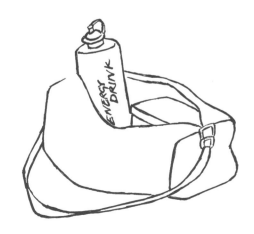

- Is it a banned substance?
- Find out all you can from a reputable source:
  - Do not just read one scientific paper.
  - Find out the whole story.
  - What does the weight of scientific evidence suggest? Go with the weight of evidence. There is little, if any, sound evidence for many products that are claimed to provide a benefit.
  - Is the research from a genuine, independent, well-known scientific centre?
  - Was it published in a well-known scientific journal?
  - Does the research apply to your discipline?
  - Do you understand fully how to use the product?
  - Is the source pure?
  - Are there any contra indications for taking it?
  - Are there any side effects?
- Do not take anything just because someone else does.
- Try to be objective in assessing any benefits or problems that you see (eg ask your performers to record training times and how they felt while trying certain substances – did they feel good/bad, how was their performance at this time?).

Finally, have you already considered all the other many factors that affect performance (eg training, diet, fluid intake, sleep pattern)? They can make a major difference to training and performance.

If you have any queries or concerns over the legality of any substances, you are advised to contact the UK Sport's Drug Information Line on 0800-528 0004.

6.5   Iron Deficiency Anaemia

Chapter 2.5 explains iron deficiency anaemia and highlights that some sports performers may be more prone to this condition than the rest of the population.

A well-trained performer has a larger blood volume than an untrained person which means that the haemoglobin is more diluted. Therefore it is fairly common for a trained performer to have a lower value of haemoglobin – which is a measure of circulating iron. There are a number of further blood tests that can be carried out by an expert to look at the iron status of the body, including ferritin. It is useful to include a measure of the ferritin level when considering the possibility of anaemia in performers as this gives a measure of the body's iron stores.

In some cases it may be necessary for individuals to take iron supplements. For instance, it may be that a teenage female performer will simply not be able to take sufficient iron on board from her diet alone. There are, however, side effects to some iron supplements (see page 10) and therefore they should be avoided if at all possible. Careful consideration should always be given to the performer's diet as it is important to make sure this is effective in the long term.

Where is Iron Found?

Iron is found in a number of foods, the richest sources being meat and meat products. There is iron in some plant foods but our bodies are not as good at taking the iron from those foods.

The iron found in plant foods is absorbed more readily if vitamin C is present in the same meal but its absorption is hindered if tannin from tea is present. There are therefore other factors to consider than just including foods that contain iron.

The following list gives some of the sources of iron which can be included in the diet. Some of these foods only contain fairly small amounts of iron but they can contribute to the iron content of the diet if used regularly.

Animal sources of iron include:

- red meat especially liver and kidney – these are the best sources of iron
- oily fish (eg sardines, pilchards, whitebait and shellfish).

Plant foods with the richest iron content include:

- breakfast cereals fortified with iron
- dried fruits (eg raisins, currants, apricots, figs)
- whole grains
- green leafy vegetables (eg spinach, spring greens, parsley, watercress)
- pulses (eg soya beans, lentils, red kidney beans, aduki beans).

Taking vitamin C with a meal will help the absorption of iron so encourage your performers to try some of the following ideas:

- Pure orange juice as a drink with meals.
- Baked beans, wholemeal bread and a kiwi fruit.
- Fortified breakfast cereal plus pure orange or grapefruit juice.

- Egg and watercress sandwiches with tomato.
- Sardines on toast with a fresh orange.

6.6   Planning

Nutrition has an important role to play in performance and should therefore be considered in the planning process. The whole team should work together to include nutrition as one of the targets for the team. Depending on the level of the performer, the team may include a doctor, physiotherapist, psychologist, physiologist, sports dietitian, parents, teachers, fitness adviser as well as the coach. As with all aspects of training the nutrition message should be consistent and sound. When planning your coaching year, consider the important aspects of nutrition for each season, training and competition period. Here are some ideas:

- Would a presentation on sport nutrition be useful during the winter training period?
- Do you have some kit bag lists ready for summer?
- Is there a list of suitable snack foods?
- Are you prepared for the track/ pool/pitch/court side questions?

NB Check your performers have the right type of foods at hand at their home and/or training base.

6.7 Elite and Recreational Performers

If you coach people of varying abilities and ambitions, it is important to distinguish the differences between them. As their coach, you should be sensitive to their individual needs and avoid the *one system for all* approach.

Elite performers are very often aware of nutrition, although that does not always mean they have got it all right. Not all elite performers have had the opportunity to gain information or may even have been misinformed.

For elite performers, good nutrition should be as much a part of their training as warming up and should be second nature. Most will be motivated to listen and react to your advice – those who are not, should be!

Recreational performers, while not under the same pressure to produce results, should still pay attention to what they eat. All performers need to supply appropriate fuel to their muscles. However, the recreational performer may not want or need to be quite so strict in their outlook to training and diet. With youngsters, for example, you may have to compromise but remember – **the right food will maximise performance at all levels.**

CHAPTER SEVEN:
Conclusion

7.0   Summary

Exercise and sport place additional and sometimes heavy demands upon the body. The body's ability to meet this demand is dependent on the availability of suitable energy sources. In addition to effective cardio-respiratory systems and the capacity to take in and use oxygen effectively, the body needs fuel. Food and drink supply this fuel.

This handbook has outlined the basic principles of nutrition for health. It has emphasised the importance of general health for sport – without it your performers are unlikely to fulfil their potential as sportspeople. You should be familiar with the various nutrients, their function and what foods they can be obtained from. However, you should now also be able to give your performers some general advice on how they can make nutrition work for them and the demands of their sport. Some of the issues surrounding food and sport have been introduced to help you identify any potential problems and know where to go for further advice.

As a coach you should be able to take these basic principles, along with the practical suggestions, and use them with your performers.

Finally, some questions you might consider include:

- are my performers drinking and eating the right foods before they come to train

- are they involved in other sports which means they are using more precious fuel

- do they bring drinks and snacks to training and competition

- are those drinks and snacks appropriate

- do they understand which are the most appropriate drinks and snacks?

Using the information in this book, you should be able to answer these questions and provide your performers with the right information.

Don't forget to look at your own eating habits and change them if necessary. It is much easier to preach what you practise and your performers will respect you more for setting a good example.

7.1 Where Next?

To help put some of the ideas in this handbook into practice, you are strongly recommended to reread any of the chapters that are particularly relevant to you and your performers. Take note of those workshops and resources recommended throughout the book. These will help to extend your knowledge further on specific topics and improve your coaching.

Recommended **sports coach UK** Develop Your Coaching Workshops and resources (complimentary with the corresponding workshop) include:

sports coach UK Develop Your Coaching Workshops	Resources
Analysing Your Coaching	Analysing Your Coaching
Coaching Children and Young People	Coaching Young Performers
Coaching Disabled Performers	Coaching Disabled Performers
Coaching Methods and Communication	The Successful Coach
Creating a Safe Coaching Environment	Creating a Safe Coaching Environment
Field-based Fitness Testing	A Guide to Field Based Fitness Testing
Fitness and Training	Physiology and Performance
Fuelling Performers	Fuelling Performers
Goal-setting and Planning	A Guide to Planning Coaching Programmes
Safeguarding and Protecting Children	Safeguarding and Protecting Children
Imagery Training	Imagery Training
Improving Practices and Skill	Improving Practices and Skill
Injury Prevention and Management	Sports Injury

sports coach UK Develop Your Coaching Workshops	Resources
Motivation and Mental Toughness	Motivation and Mental Toughness
Performance Profiling	Performance Profiling (audiotape and booklet)

Details of all sports coach UK resources are available from:

Coachwise 1st4sport
Chelsea Close
Off Amberley Road
Armley
Leeds LS12 4HP
Tel: 0113-201 5555
Fax: 0113-231 9606
Email: enquiries@1st4sport.com
Website: www.1st4sport.com

sports coach UK also produces a technical journal, *coaching edge* formerly known as *Faster, Higher, Stronger (FHS)*. Details of these are available from:

sports coach UK
114 Cardigan Road
Headingley
Leeds LS6 3BJ
Tel: 0113-274 4802
Fax: 0113-275 5019
Email: coaching@sportscoachuk.org
Website: www.sportscoachuk.org

For further details of sports coach UK workshops in your area, contact the sports coach UK Business Support Centre (BSC):

sports coach UK
Business Support Centre
Sports Development Centre
Loughborough University
Loughborough
Leicestershire LE11 3TU
Tel: 01509-226 130
Fax: 01509-226 134
Email: bsc@sportscoachuk.org
Website: www.sportscoachuk.org/improve/workshop/search.asp

Sports Council for Wales

Tel: 0845-045 0904
Fax: 029-2030 0600
Email: scw@scw.co.uk
Website: www.sports-council-wales.co.uk

Sports Council for Northern Ireland

Tel: 028-9038 1222
Fax: 028-9068 2757
Email: info@sportni.net
Website: www.sportni.net

sportscotland

Tel: 0131-317 7200
Fax: 0131-317 7202
Email: library@sportscotland.org.uk
Website: www.sportscotland.org.uk

7.2   Suggested Further Reading

Bean, Anita (1996) *The Complete Guide to Sports Nutrition.* 2nd Edition. London: A & C Black. ISBN: 0-71364-388-9

Thompson, Ron A and Sherman, Roberta T (1992) *Helping Athletes with Eating Disorders.* Champaign, IL: Human Kinetics. ISBN: 0-87322-383-7

Williams, Clyde and Devlin, John T (1992) *Foods, Nutrition and Sports Performance.* London: Spon Press. ISBN: 0-419-17890-2

Williams, Melvin H (1997) *The Ergogenics Edge: Pushing the Limits of Sports Performance.* Champaign, IL: Human Kinetics. ISBN: 0-88011-545-9

7.3   Useful Addresses

If your performer needs more detailed advice, a list of accredited sports dietitians can be obtained from:

Dietitians in Sport and
Exercise Nutrition (DISEN)
PO Box 22360
London W13 9FL

For advice on eating disorders, contact:

Beat eating Disorders Association
(EDA)
103 Prince of Wales Road
Norwich NR1 1DW

This association operates a Helpline on 0845-634 1414 and a Youth Helpline on 0845-634 7650.

A

B

C

D

Index

Mission Statement

sports coach UK is dedicated to guiding the development and implementation of a coaching system, recognised as a world leader, for all coaches at every level in the UK.

We will work with our partners to achieve this, by promoting:

- professional and ethical values
- inclusive and equitable practice
- agreed national standards of competence as a benchmark at all levels
- a regulated and licensed structure
- recognition, value and appropriate funding and reward
- a culture and structure of innovation, constant renewal and continuous professional development (CPD).

The **sports coach UK** mission statement is likely to be reviewed in the context of the Coaching Framework.